ALEXANDER IRVING'S

"CURTAIN RISING"

Watermeadow

1

This edition first published in 2005
by Watermeadow
Sherborne-St-John Hampshire RG24 9HY

Typeset by Wyeth Group Limited
Printed and bound in England by Wyeth Group Limited

Alexander Irving is hereby identified as author of this work in
accordance with section 77 of the Copyright,
Designs and Patents Act 1988

A CIP record for this book
is available from the British Library

ISBN 0-9549639-0-3 (pbk)

EDITOR'S INTRODUCTION

"Curtain Rising" is the first published work of Alexander Irving's poetry. That this work is identified as more than an anthology is strongly apparent. Rather the poems together can be considered as a unique totality based on a fully developed motif.

The work as a whole represents Man's journey from darkness into light. This process is characterised in stages: successively, the self-elevation of Man as his own deity, the intrinsic power of latent primordial forces to influence the psyche, the chosen release from the bounds of a cynical and corrupt world system of governance, rules and heredity, the subsequent confrontation with the personal forces released when alone, the forging of self-identity and the removal of "masks", the realisation of choice and the continued existence of evil, the recognition of the state of Man as a fallen being, and the redemptive state of the path "home" where Man is in balance with God, evil, and himself.

That Alexander Irving has tackled these immense subjects in his first work, and at his age, is indeed commendable. What is, however, truly extraordinary is the depth with which he has penetrated and analysed the core of the problems associated with the human condition. Man's relationship with his own nature, the realisation of the actuality of the "Fall", the identification of motive impulses and their power, the construction of the moral choice, the rejection of cynicism, the final reconciliation between the forces of good and evil, and the conclusive recognition that evil (and therefore doubt) cannot be destroyed but can be contained and defeated through Faith in God.

What characterises "Curtain Rising" is the strength of emotion conveyed in image. This imagery transcends mere simple words to allow the work to reveal the profundity of its message-which runs as a constant theme throughout.

The work as a whole eschews rationalism and cynicism and relies heavily on human emotions and senses. The perceptions resulting from this methodology allow the many apparent inversions in thought to truly elucidate and expand the problems presented in a way that a logical approach would surely have failed. Running right throughout the whole work is the contrast of choice and the duality of Man's condition, as the mechanism of the main themes. The final reconciliation of the generated tensions leaves no introduced avenue unexplored and un-resolved.

Above all one is left with the unmistakable belief that Alexander Irving has created in " Curtain Rising" a substantive, unifying and undeniably emotional work. For an author of Alexander Irving's age to have produced such a profound and complete study in his first work is truly an outstanding achievement.

THE STRUCTURE OF "CURTAIN RISING"

In order to facilitate the study of the work as a whole it is perhaps helpful to consider the overall structure as being composed of twelve thematic areas.

Part i: The Eternal Recurrence of the Problem of Man (and the Solution)

Part ii: The Fall

Part iii: The Effect of Cynical Rationalism on the Individual

Part iv: Anxiety and Impulse

Part v: Recognition and Dilemma

Part vi: Being Alone and the Power of Pain.

            The Duality of Self

            The Power of Anger

Part vii: The Awakening

Part viii: Repentance

Part ix: Redemption of Self

Part x: The Ignorance of Cynicism

Part xi: Doubt

Part xii: Home

THE STYLE OF "CURTAIN RISING"

The symmetry of the above structure has allowed Alexander Irving to construct "Curtain Rising" in an highly formal and architectural style.

It can be stated that the overall style employs simple but effective words that convey direct images and set an atmosphere that is relevant to the meaning of the text.

It is interesting to identify just some of the techniques that Alexander Irving uses to create a sense of formal unity in the whole work:

(i) to utilise the same material, but in different structural contexts in different poems, provides a link in variety.

e.g   seas, lakes, ponds, water, waves, crystals, dancing, serpents, wolves, fire, sun, light, silence, shadows, cracks, colours, dreams, gold, home, rain and memories.

(ii) the powerful invocation of unified thematic meaning through the choice of the titles of individual poems and the various and contrasting constructions of parallel meaning in the poem itself.

e.g   whilst "TOTAL ECLIPSE" as a poem title invokes the physical creation of full darkness on earth (when the sun's light rays are still present) which creates the generic image of the victory of evil over goodness being total but temporary (the moon passes), one of the principal lines in the same poem states:

"Going are the times when Man looked down"- this invokes the past image of Man in purity but now eclipsed in sin, and/or central Man is "fallen" with no light (eclipsed), and/or a direct reference to Jesus (Son of Man) at the crucifixion, and/or (without any reference to the title of the poem) Man has ceased to be afraid of God. All are applicable.

Such a technique produces a complexity and augmented profundity of meaning that only enhances in a noble fashion the duality of the message that Alexander Irving is attempting to construct.

(iii) A further technique that Alexander Irving frequently uses is to take the sensory mechanisms (of colour sight for example) and project them out to an external object, which is of course the reverse of the reception of sensory data (where light is received from the object), and then to transfigure the projection to, for example, the embodiment of sin. This allows Man to be at the centre, and the world around him just a manifestation of his evil desires, lit from within as opposed to from without. When, as in "Perception", this manifestation gradually disappears into "but we are alone...no you. Just me" we are left in no doubt that Man is at the centre of the universe, there is no God, there is evil, there are no human relationships-and there is nothing else. Through this technique the poem portrays an ominous sense of power and despair-with Man at the centre.

This is an extraordinary powerful technique for a first work.

One also notices that Alexander Irving always deals in the primary colours-never "white" light.

This reveals Man as a refractive character who separates the incoming and given purity into component parts for his own purposes.

(iv) In many instances Alexander Irving uses the technique of the inverted symbol in a powerful framework of images. The "Hangman"(the devil), for example, lies in wait for the Man who has taken the wrong choice (" an easy way for the blind to go, a clever path for the fools who know") producing and inviting an "opening of the eyes of night" and the "black embrace". We find, however, that as Man waits for the "dawn":

"The time has come to close your eyes
but still come the wind and rain
for the one who will be along
is the hangman in you and me"

With this technique, the external punisher (The Hangman), the One who takes away our lives, on the "clever path", is actually inside all of us and preventing any awakening. The mechanism of this awareness is caused by the vivid interplay of changing contrasts that are locked around a central theme.

In order to add irony to the symbolic image of perpetual living death, Man is observed opening his eyes into the night ("she came to me with a serpent's kiss "), although "blind", and closing them into the dawn ("eye of the sun").

This complex interplay of images and symbolism leaves us in no doubt that Man's constitution is such that it difficult to understand how he can extricate himself from the 'Fallen' condition.

It is this image of Man in a continued "Fall" that marks the central point of "Curtain Rising"-from this state the recapitulation will be to travel "home". The mechanism and catalyst that Alexander Irving employs for this "travel" is the recognition of good as a cognitive purpose in Man, and the anger associated with the co-existence of evil and the cynicism of fallen Man's moral condition. This tension is prevalent throughout the whole structure and style of "Curtain Rising"

(v) Throughout the whole work Alexander Irving is creating the developing image of the pyschological construction of Man. In the beginning is the pure Unity of the Word, from which Man departs, and thus develops the repressed "shadow" of the unconscious. Man, becomes aware of the resident existence of deep instinctive forces that impulse to embrace evil, and develops a personality "mask" to run-away. An escape (from both good and evil) to establish a relative system based on cynical absolutes.

From within this primordial mess, however, we see the rise of the individual Will - the Soul - to seek goodness in the face of evil.

The tension in "Curtain Rising" is caused by the determination of the evolving Will to cross the "wall", the "locked door", (as a cognitive act of purpose) to absorb and give goodness. This involves the angry stripping away of the societal "cloak" and the "legacy of Adam".

It is the evolution of the individual Will, against both the prevailing evil inherent in mankind and the cynicism of society, towards the Unity of the Word - God's Will – that is the battleground of "Curtain Rising".

(vi) In the final redemptive state of Man, Alexander Irving leaves us in no doubt that Man's condition has not changed ("I vs Me") but his power of choice has. For example, in "The Midnight Sun", Jesus can be seen and heard in the blackness of evil:

" I can see you
the light in the dark
your noisy silence
faces the midnight sun"

In these later poems the language assumes a simplicity of its own with calm contrasts. The "Me" is dropped and the "I" becomes aware of the "Father of my dreams"-a concise quote to state the acceptance of God's Grace over the motive forces of the subconscious forces of Man. In other words evil has not gone anywhere –but it is controllable.

We notice the opposite logic attached to good and evil.

The "midnight sun"-the light in the darkness- contrasting with the "total eclipse"-the darkness caused by the full prevention of light access by the obstacle (moon).

This represents the transfiguration of the physically defined obstacle to an ubiquitous darkness where the light is still present and attainable through choice.

(vii) The co-existence of good and evil runs as a central theme throughout "Curtain Rising." Alexander Irving, however, introduces this motive in a number of interesting ways.

For example, in "Simplicity":

"He celebrated his freedom
as he swam on the lake
coming out crystal clear
with a jubilant look on his face"

Alexander Irving has subsequently taken "crystal clear" (free from sin) - which refers to Man's state ("on the lake") before the Fall (Part 1) - and created the dialectical structure of "The Crystal Lake" (Part 11) – a shocking depiction of Man's actual condition without God:

"The air tastes like wine
as the dragonflies
skim the crystal water

but do not disturb the surface
they don't know what lies beneath:
Bodies decaying
Rotting
Thousands of them: rotting"

One should not forget, however, that within the body of the unified work there are individual poems, that, in themselves, can be considered as powerful self-contained works.

Whilst it may be somewhat irregular in a work of unity to point out a number of poems that, through their own unique style, construction and depth, would attract considerable merit, it is important to recognise that there is a considerable latent talent at work in their construction.

Many of the poems are characterised by a very noble, classical and romantic structure.

Truly, "Curtain Rising" can be considered as a powerful first work.

CONTENTS of "CURTAIN RISING"

TOTAL ECLIPSE

Cold as steel the darkness waits
its hour will come
Mother nature's black revenge
on those who waste her life
She'll turn our ashes to ice.

Around the world the people stop
with terror stricken eyes
A shadow cast upon us all
In the icy rain and whiplashed seas
There's nowhere left to run.

Around the world the nations wait
For some wise words from their leading light
It's not only madmen who listen to fools
" Is this the end?" millions cried
clutching their riches as they died.

Going are the days when man looks down
        our time is ending
to be set free it took so long.
It's not the journey's end
        It's just begun.

SIMPLICITY

The man who lived in the tree
threw a goblet in the air
it turned and spiralled
and melted into liquid.

The drop of gold
folded down his cheek
and the remains exploded
in a shower of colours.

The man who lived in the tree
danced under the shower of gold
he was finally free
from the goblet's holding power.

He had tried for so long
to be set free
to live like the Theoxenia(1)
but the goblet had stopped him.

Now the goblet lay in shards
scattered on the floor
the man was free
and he danced and he cried.

He celebrated his freedom
as he swam on the lake
coming out crystal clear
with a jubilant look on his face.

He is free.

The man who lived in the tree
Turns around and runs to his home
And enters the tree
And closes the door
With a red nob and welcome mat outside
he enters the house
Where there is nothing
But him.

(1) The notes of Alexander Irving indicate that
Theoxenia is perhaps the word the author intended.
This is a festival ("entertainments given to the
gods") celebrated in many parts of Greece, not only
of the principal local divinity, but of many others
who were considered as his guests. Such was the
feast held at Delphi in honour of Apollo in the
month hence called Theoxenios (August)

ETERNAL

The bird flies
and it can't avoid the sight
it flies through the serpent in the sky
the beak slices through the serpent's skin
making room for the head

The serpent writhes in pain
and its forked tongue
flinches and falls
as the bird
squirms through the hole
thrashing, smashing
making the hole big enough

Dark clouds form over the sight
and the rain begins to fall
the bird rolls and twists
advancing into the hole
a roll of thunder
a fork of lightening
as the serpent shrieks in horror

This struggle covers
all the earth
the Parthenon and Mecca
the Ganges to the Thames
the Somme to the ganglands
People of all creeds and colours
have seen this flight

and people of all creeds and colours
have felt its might.

The beak emerges
on the other side
and the people of the world
turn away
as the serpent flings back its head
silhouetted by the lightening
and lets out its last howl

As the serpent falls to the ground
the people fall to their knees
and let out a cry
as the serpent lies
rain hating its brow
a tear comes to its eye.
The serpent dissolves to black

The bird lands on a bleak tree
and in a moment
the metamorphosis is complete
and the bird is a serpent
writhing on the empty branches
and it grows,
it grows
until it slithers into the sky
floating on the winds
one serpent is replaced by another
and the people turn
and walk away
leaving serpent
hovering above them
framed against the brooding sky.
The cycle has come
full circle once more.

A GRAVE NEW WORLD

Take a walk through the world today!
Just what do you expect to see?
It's just a vast expanse of grey
stretching from the land to the sea.
As the wind blows over the barren land
time seems unemployed
and it stretches out a cold, wispy hand
to pull us with it, into the void.
Look, from horizon to horizon
the colour is bleak and grim
as time's hand is turned.

Ruins of the old world order
strewn across the ground
the glory of the battle called her
a peaceful solution was never found.
In the streets the babies are burned!
they plunged from heaven down to hell
left with an eerie reminder
and a vicious tale to tell
of mother nature when her anger did bind her!
There can be no error,
they were stranded in a sea of terror.

But just when all seemed over
colours spring from the grey, grisly, ground
yellow and red and a four-leaved clover
as the remaining few gathered round.
Sunlight oozed into the grey air,
as honey drips from a spoon,
the colours spread without care
to ensure that soon
the world would be covered.
Time springs back to life
never again its course deferred.

A rainbow of emotion greets the pardoned
She allows a second chance
but the warning has been given
with the wind and the rain
how long till we incur
Her wrath and terror again?

THE CRYSTAL LAKE

It shimmers like a roll of silver
Dazzling light springs from the surface
Green light and blue
Shine from the depths
Winking like cat's eyes.

It rolls into the distance
a constant soothing lapping
on the golden shores
the emerald water
flows and ebbs away.

The air tastes like wine
as the dragonflies
skim the crystal water
but do not disturb the surface
they don't know what lies beneath:

Bodies decaying
Rotting
Thousands of them: rotting,
Half decomposed
The skin being eaten away.

Thousands of them: motionless
lying there, lifeless,
rotting away
The water is murky
with human skin.

Inside the crystal lake
Full of decay
Lurking beneath the surface
Of those emerald ripples
Is a rotting world.

One that we know of:
but just can't see.

MY MUSE

She dances on a ring of fire
Silhouetting her form against the wall
She dances alone
framed by the flames
all heads turn to watch her
as she dances out her song.

You can sense her presence
as she dances her heat
as the flames lick higher
the world will take notice
of the un-named girl
in the ring of flame.

"She dances that which is known
She dances that which is unknown
and in between are the doors"
Linking the un-lockable
that she has flung open for me.

PERCEPTION

I have colours swirling behind my eyes
the wolf in the distance makes no sound
as red, yellow and green
curl around the wolf
surrounding him
binding him

A tear comes to my eye
subconscious flooding through
a wave of orange
a flash of red
turn and burn
all in my head

The wolf howls at the night
at the twirling serpent's plight
and all is just right
as the snake twirls and curls
around the wolf
surrounding him
binding him.

Magenta
Magnolia
comes over her
the glorious ballroom dancer
who with a shake of a leg
is away

Red and yellow
green and brown

She dances in a ring of fire
nothing to quench her desire
to be at one with the wolf
to experience its plight
to be in the fight.

She carries a head of despair
and all else fades to the air
in colours of gold and silver
she is bound
and burned in the furnaces
of red.

Now all is black
And the snake curls around that tree
that is you and me
the tree is sparse
and she, the wolf, the snake
you and me
turn as one
to face the sun
but we are alone
no she, no wolf, no snake
no you.
Just me.

........THE PLACE WHERE NO MEN LIVE

As the wind blows over the barren land
time seems unemployed
the endless desolate horizon
stretches out like a bleak carpet
in the place where no men live.

A man approaches from across the horizon
so pale he looks like death itself
the skin peals off his face
ashamed of its owner
in the place where no men live.

He looks around at the destruction
a tear comes to his shallow eye
it rolls down his cheek, he licks, drinks
completing the cycle
in the place where no men live.

He continues his endless steps
the life he's chosen, the life he now leads
he, the causer of this destruction
knows it was his error
in the place where no men live.

The sun like a fading rose
shall no longer rise
as it falls below the horizon
silhouetted on a hill, to greet the last remaining night
in the place where no men live.

"wisdom is by far the greatest part of joy
the words of the proud

paid for in the blood of men
with the mighty blows of fate
which at long last
will teach us wisdom"
on earth where no men live.

QUARTET IN A

Looking up from the gutter I see
The world as it is to be
No putrid, deranged, rabid flea
Sucks, draws and expires on me.

THE LEGACY OF ADAM

If you look across the world today
what do you expect to see?
No longer do we have green fields
or tall trees.
We have
a bleak horizon
a dark reminder
of what is to come.

We are a fallen people.
We are a race who have failed
and as I get somewhat older
I get a little less wise.
As the world pollutes me
day by day
I am corrupted more.
What bliss ignorance must have been.
But as I learn more
I find I know less

How easy it would be
to hate goodness.
How easy it would be
to despise morality.
How hard it is
to abhor evil
in the world we live.

As I get older
I get more cynical
Doubting even Your light
Can shine on a world such as this.
Or will it be like me
Engulfed by the darkness?
I am left
On my bed
In solitary despair.

THE SHADOW

Hands in pockets
go through the park
quicken the pace
the night is dark

The wind through the trees
Fear
The unexplained noise
Fear
The footsteps from behind
Fear

The shadow roams into view
given life by the streetlight
the shadow is large
It's dark
It's menacing
It's getting closer
I quicken my pace
It's getting closer
  Closer
   Closer
         Two feet
        One foot
             Overtaken.

A man like me
scared of a shadow
and just trying to get home.

THE CLOAK

The toothless, sweaty, senile
Old Man
Arises from his chair
Bumbling
Mumbling
Above his head he lifts a cloak
A crooked smile greets his lips
He places the cloak on me
I strive, I strain
The cloak will not cover me
All your life it will never,
Never be enough.
Fighting, striving,
Stretching, the cloak
But it only covers your head
      Failure
      Useless
      Rejection
The toothless, sweaty, senile
      Old Man has won
Sitting in his chair
      Bumbling
      Mumbling.

JUST DUST

You think your're important
You think your're something special
but your're just the same as me
just dust and bones

Those who are proud will pay
so roll on judgement day
Your time will come
then you will get that back seat feeling

Your're not important
Your're nothing special
from dust you were crafted
and to dust you will return.

AMBITION

This will have no hidden meaning
This will have no higher level
This is how you see it
This is frustration printed on a page.

Imagine if you will
that you have a dream
a desire that burns inside
and as each day passes you want it more and more
but you know you cannot have it
and it gnaws you from inside to out.

This is how I live
That is how I'll die
and that is how I'll continue
so come the fog and the rain.

Could it be
that He
is doing this to me
as part of a game?
He has planted the desire
the need
to have my dream
but has not given me
the abilities to succeed.

I don't want to believe that my God
would do that to me
but could it be that as my frustration rages
He steps back, and laughs at me.

I can feel the anger inside
as it changes me
and eats me away
I become bitter
I become sour
I become rotten
as my dream
Is denied to me.

And so I stand alone
drowning in a pool of frustration
my dream behind a door
and He has the key.

So the dream
remains the dream
locked away
denied to me
never to be
Reality.

SHAME

It clings to me like a wet shirt
it will not let me free
I try to release myself from its grip
but its hold only tightens around me.

My sins God cannot want.
Someone so perfect
I cannot pollute
so bear with me as I reflect

Power sapping
strength tapping
struggling to understand
this hole I am in

Ashamed of my shame
cannot give it away
the cycle is long and hard
the cycle makes me.

I'm frantic in your soothing arms
I can now tell what I must do
So I will remove myself from sight
leave hope, exit light
as with the darkness of my soul
I become another shadow
that makes up the night.

TIDES

I look ahead,
I see a narrow road,
a gradient steep.
My life stretches in front,
like a book
I already know the ending.

The sting is taken out of death
by the fact that I know
there is nothing I can do.
So I follow my pre-determined life,
like a dog and its master,
to the end of the line.

This should be nothing new,
You knew it would end like that.
It is just a question of when,
like a date on the calendar,
or will I take even God
by surprise?

I know I will die,
so will you,
It is all I am certain of.
I am but a blink of an eye,
like a turn of the head,
a speck in the world.

What difference will I make?
What purpose do I have?
Am I here to live my own way?
I think not.

But it is not to be thought about now,
as I turn out the light,
On another day of my life.

HARD TIMES

Is this what has become of me?
Sitting at my desk
with half- read books,
    Half-finished essays
cluttered all around me.

I work to get the grades
but in the end
they mean nothing.
They slap a label
but it is not me.

I spend my life examining the works of others
as my own works shrivel and die.
The rose has gone
and left just the thorn
that cuts deep inside me.

I am three hours from sleep
back to the reality -
that is me.
When asleep I know who I am.
Everything so clear - perfect clarity.

RED AND YELLOW

Swirling red and yellow
drift behind my eyes
imagination on a ball and chain
never to be freed

All I am not
is all I want
this planted ambition
with no means for success

Such relentless pressure
the will,
the drive for success
trying to be someone else

This is about the never - ending night
that is me
as I push,
I strive,
I strain,
but ultimately,
I will fail.

UNSETTLING THE INNER SANCTUM

Looking from side to side
my time I must bide
creep around the corner
my shadow seems smaller

All is dark
the distance fields: a lark
the thick air
I must bare

From behind me I hear
a twig snaps very near
I turn to see
but no figure is apparent to me.

I continue my steps
Matched by my breaths
Another twig breaks
The noise as deadly as snakes

I turn, I see
a dark figure
he brandishes a knife
and plunges it into my flesh.

Collapsing to the ground
lying dead
my eyes flicker open
to regain my place.
In the living dead.

APOCALYPSE NOW, PLEASE

I hate what the world has made of me
    so useless
    so downtrodden
    so corrupt
and I cannot stand to grow up
    in a world like this.

What have we done?
How did it come to this?
Why is God allowing this?

Can't He send a flood
    To drown us all
    Leave none alive
Can't He kill us all?

Thank the heavens
I am not God
Such power,
matched with my rage,
thank the heavens God is more forgiving
than me.

We are a fallen race-
a people who have failed.
I take a step back and start to laugh
You know we can never last!

THE VOICE OF SILENCE

This is the voice of silence
that is screaming to you
this is the voice of silence
can you hear it too?

This is the pain
that keeps you down
this is the pain
that will make you want to drown.

This is the burden of every man
that is the rejector
this is the burden of every man
the final infector.

This is the voice of silence
can you hear it too?
this is the voice of silence
listen carefully
it's screaming to you.

THE POOL

Take a look in this pool
and what do you see?
In the dark depths
there are faces beckoning me
Can't you see them?
It's plain for me to see
they were there - I know you don't believe me.

I've never felt so strange
but I'm not going insane
I've no doubt that you
think I'm off my head
You don't say but it's in your eyes, instead
Hours I spend just gazing in the pool
They just draw me there - I don't know what to do.

They draw my strength away
ther're asking me to stay
nightmares, spirits, calling me
they can't leave me be
all my life blood is slowly draining away
and I feel I'm weaker every day
I know I haven't long to go - joining them at the
bottom of the pool.

Now I feel they are so near
I begin to see them – very clear
nightmares coming all the time
will wreck your (fragile) peace of mind.

Now it's clear
and I know what I must do
I must take you there
to look at them too
hand in hand we'll jump right in that pool
can't you see - it's not just me
they want you too!

We'll drown together
and we'll be forever
in nightmares
forever
calling me
now I never
rest in peace.

THE TRIBE OF WANNADU

In a time when discoverers walked the earth
When the land (was) swamp and (the) caves were
home
In an age when fire was the prize possession
To search the landscapes men would roam.

Then the tribes they came to steal their fire
and the wolves howled into the night
as they fought a vicious battle
to save the power of warmth and light.

And when the embers died away,
They thought the flame of life had burnt and died
They didn't know the sparks that made the fire
were made by rubbery stick and stone.

So they ploughed through forest and swamp
They fought the cannibal tribes and beasts
In the search to find another fire
To regain the power of light and heat.

The Wannadu (are) now no more
they (in fear) scoured the land
in (the) search (whilst on) their roam
stick and stone lay (unused) at home.

THE CROSS

Eleven saintly shrouded men
Silhouettes stand against the sky
One in front with a cross held high
Come to wash my sins away

Standing alone in the wind and the rain
Feeling the fear that is growing
Sensing the change again
By the storm that is brewing.
Some of the doubt in the things you believe
Now that your faith will be put to the test
Nothing to do but await the fear
The fear that is growing

Why is God still protecting me?
Even when I don't deserve it
Though I'm blessed with inner strength
Why am I meant to face this alone?
Asking the question
Time and time again
Praying to God: "keep me alive."
Inside my head: I feel the fear rise

They'll be saying their prayers
When the moment comes
There'll be penance to pay
When its judgement day
The guilty will bleed
Coming to claim
Take your soul away

They'll be coming
To bring the eternal flame
Bring us all immortality
Holding the Communion
So the world would be blessed
My creator, my God,
My God 'll lay my soul to rest

Lost the love of heaven above
Chose the lust of the earth below
Come you eleven saintly shrouded men
Come wash my sins away

TAKEN FROM US

Sky scrapers towering high
Great works of art standing proud
The beauty of nature by and by
The ethnical, rich clustered crowd
Melt away
To portray
What life is.
Life is not glamorous showbiz
Where all is fair and free is all
Life is completely cruel.
The most wonderfulness you could ever meet,
So kind,
So generous,
So absolutely pure,
Not a bad bone in her malfunctioning body,
She always strived to give,
But she's been taken from us.
First mind,
Then breath,
Then heart,
Stopped in turn.
As the life-support machine is rested
She is taken from us.
The good always perish first
There will never be anyone else like you
Your death made me cry
For the first time in years.
I loved you
But I didn't know how much till now.

ROUTINE

All my life
I have followed a routine
certain time, certain place
they say "jump"
I say "how high"?
But now it seems
that my eyes have opened
and I have to break away.
I must escape the routine
To run free.

I am still in a cage.
Freedom is
but a notion
a glossed up cage
but it is still a cage.
My life planned out before me
based on routine
ending in death.
My aim is to earn a pound or two
I am trapped by this routine.

There is no freedom
all we choose is routine
our routine till we die
there is no other option,
To run the routine.
To earn a pound or two
until my scheduled death.

INNOCENT AND YOUNG

I hid inside my world
I took what I could find
I cried when I was lonely
I felt down when I was bad

How can I ever satisfy you?
How can I ever make you see?
Inside we are all somebody else
It does not matter what you want to be

But now I got to smile
I hope you can comprehend
But anything can happen, it's time to be condemned
I step into your world
I kick you in your mind
I'm the only witness to the nature of my crime

Look at what (you've) done
To the innocent and young
Don't listen to me talk- I'm not the only one
Trash from the body-sorted by the brain
It sends tears from my conscience
Won't you tell me who's to blame?

THE MEMORY

Days may come and go
but each one goes so slow
and deep inside my head
I can't remember what you said
like the threads that spiders throw
memories, like days, come and go.

I wish that summer would melt to winter
and once again the cold would splinter
through our hearts and minds
to unlock your crimes
But yet.......I know it will not be
And the memory is taunting me.

What was it you said?
what was that, it entered my head?

Hold it fast!
No, I let it past
I feel it burning the tip of my tongue
but in my head a well placed bung.

Now the trees stand sparse
now there's (less) green in the grass
now that winter has come back
to this memory help me track!

Now I remember what you said
I remember now and will make you pay!
You said......"have a nice day."

RE-LOAD

What you did to me cannot be forgotten
but it can be forgiven.
The thought moves with a slide and a slither
and trailing behind it a mucous river.

But later in the evening
as I lay awake in bed
with the echoes of the past day ringing in my head
and in a moment
the memory of all that remains
not even every minute time contains
would be enough to stop the pain,
and all the wounds are re-opened again.

THE SECRET OF THE HANGMAN

O God of Earth and Altar,
bow down and hear our cry,
Our earthly rules falter,
Our people drift and die.
The walls of gold entomb us
the swords of scorn divide
take not thy thunder from us
but take away my pride.

Just a babe in a black abyss
no reason for a place like this,
the walls are cold and cry in pain.
An easy way for the blind to go
a clever path for the fools who know.
The secret of the hangman, the smile on his lips,
the light of the blind, the venom that tears my spine,
the eyes of night are opening.
She came to me with a serpent's kiss
as the eye of the sun rose on her lips
moonlight catches the silver tears I cry.
So we lay on a black embrace
and the seed is sown in the holy place
and I watched and waited for the dawn.
Bind us all together, ablaze with hope and fear,
no storm or heavy weather will rock our boat.
The time has come to close your eyes
but still come the wind and rain
for the one who will be along
is the hangman in you and me.

INSIDE

I'm spiralling down
So come. Watch me drown.
As I slip into the underworld
Not noticed: laying curled.
Examining myself closely
What is it that makes me?
Outside my head: enemies in disguise
Inside: I feel the demons rise.

All I want is all I lack
Around me: my world turns black.
So, give in to your worst phobia
It's a crazy man's utopia.

Inside my mind: smoke rises in a wind
and all you thought you knew
can be swept away
by fate's cold hand.

SEASONS

Seasons don't change
they just glide through my eyes
like a serpent in the sky
tempestuous love passing me by.

Infinity of space
destroys the special place
a momentary bliss
it's the thorn in a kiss.

Seducers and you
have become my perfect two
In a world I divide
what is good and what I do.

THE DARK SIDE

I fear to close my eyes
to release the demons
that live inside my head
I fear to sleep
I fear to let down my guard
if I do, they will get in
and rip and rape and destroy.

The dark side of the mind
the hideousness it creates
the black death it creates
whose hand is on my shoulder.

The slow suicide of sleep,
each time I sleep
I hurt a little more
every sleeping breath I take
I die a little more.
Can something not save me?
I am under attack constantly
having to face this alone.

The hordes of the evil one
take a hold of my dreams
I can feel them creeping into my waking moments.
        No more.
They have taken hold
of my sleepy self
but they will not take me.

I grip my head
in an attempt to squeeze them out
those white jarring teeth
those red glaring eyes
those powerful hands
that close around my throat.
They try to force me
to force me to go with them.

They torment my dreams
they torture me
I am faced against the wolves
I am lost on a black sea of terror
I call for aid
but I am alone.

THE WRECKERS

My eyes seek reality
My fingers feel for faith
Touch clear with a dirty hand
I fall because I've let go

All I want from you is what is mine
I cry to the alleyway, confess all to the rain
But I lie straight to the mirror
Is nowhere safe from the storm?

But I can't bear to see
what will become of me
So beaten, so torn
So wicked, so worn.

But I hope you will see
That you can't cry for me
For no man is doomed.

I vs ME

I'm running out of time,
I'm running out of breath.
And now it's getting that I cannot sleep at night
In the day I feel like death.

I'm prepared.
I'm ready to fight.
To fight away myself
The part of me where evil burns bright.

I'm getting in too deep - I feel me closing in.
I've got to say I'm scared - I know that I will win.
Even so
I'll fight on.

It is I versus Me.
Good versus evil.
one must win
and only time will tell.

This will be a constant battle - but I'm ready to fight
it.
To push back evil - to bring forth the good.
In the battlefield
That is me.

LONLINESS OF A SLAVE

In my hour of need
I turn to look for support
No-one is there

Alone in the darkness
I called for a light
No-body came

Alone on a sea of fire
I cry for water
No-help came

I am dying by the hour
Getting weaker every way
As I watch the clock
Tick my life away
Without a care
One second at a time
And I turn
I am a-lone.

MEMORIES

It is hard to understand.
It is hard to comprehend;
something so final,
so infinite,
as death.

Never to look on my friend's face again.
Never to see his smile again.
But memories are all I have
and they do no justice
to who you were.

I'm finding it hard
to picture his face
as he slips out of time.
He passes out of my mind as he slips away:
away from me again.

METAMORPHOSIS

It is hard to understand.
It is hard to comprehend
something as final
as infinite
as perfectly intimate
as death.
Never to look on my friend's face again.
Never to see his smile again.
The morning sun seems colder
as memories are all I have
and still they do no justice
to who you were.
As the days go on
a transformation occurs behind my eyes
as the smiling face of my friend
is replaced with the mask of a mocking clown,
as every drop of flame
lights a candle in.
Memory of the one
who lives inside my skin
the metamorphosis is complete.
I am left in a black sea of terror
with the clown's mocking mask
always on the horizon,
as my friend's face
slips out of time and space.
As the clown laughs
he slips away
away from me again.

ME

The waves come crashing
against the rocks
with unstoppable force
like the failure that
awaits me.
I am the one
Who will work all his life
I am the one
Who would take a bullet for a friend
I am the one who is forgotten.
Such total inadequacy.
I work for all
And achieve nothing
It is all
I can expect.
Sometimes I feel
like God's little boy
that he can prod at,
and watch go
by and by.

THE FUN'S OVER

I have taken all I can
Leave me alone
Let me be.
Like a saturated sponge
I will start to ooze anger.

Enough's enough.

ANGER

Anger is a gift with which
we vent over our most powerful emotions
to purge the soul
to free the mind.

It is so misunderstood
so abused
and so misused.
It is not a destructive force.

I keep on searching for the right way to live
and I will let my anger lead me. Can you not see?
Used in the right way anger is a blessing.
A gift to the confused.

Use it the right way,
Use it to lead you.
Do not give in
And you will go far.

PENT UP FURY

Such raw aggression
such unbridled hate.
Release me now
I feel like screaming
at the top of my lungs.
I open my mouth
yet no sound comes out.

All is lost.
We are a fallen race.
All is gone.
Time has moved on.
I despair for us all.
Why is God allowing this?

Why doesn't he kill us all?
I hate the human race.
I hate us all.
I hate what we do.
Thank the heavens
I am not God.
That power,
matched with my rage,
thank heavens
God is more forgiving than me.

I take a step back - and start to laugh
You know - we can never last.

THE MASK

This is the cloud that swallows trust
This is the black that encumbers us
This is the face that you hide from
This is the mask that comes undone

Are we the people?
The people to lead a revolution?
Are we the people?
Come with me
Come with me now
Come with me now and remove your mask

Things will be all right
Look, my mask is off too
But my reflection in the window looks different.
Am I who I think I am?
I'm looking different than me

Maybe I've been doing the devil's dance too long
I look out of the window; it's all gone wrong.
    Court is in succession:
    Rip off the mask
    Reveal yourself
Slam the gavel down.

SHADOW ON THE SUN

Once upon a time
I was of the piece of mind
to lay your burden down
and leave you where you stood
You'd seen it done before
I could tell you what you saw
and never say a word
now all that is gone, over with and done
- never to return

Shapes of every size
move behind my eyes
doors inside my head
bolted from within
Every drop of flame
Lights a candle in
Memory of the one
who lives inside my skin

SILENT SACRIFICE

Another knock comes
I cry out to the page
No want for human conflict
to calm my rage.

I purge my soul through writing
Cleanse my self with ink
I know it may not be healthy
but no one
shall ever know me.

I'll tell all to the paper
confer all to the page
those who are my friends
I offer a silent apology.

The page is my escape
it becomes my sacrifice
with my pen as my tool.
To gain redemption
through the scratching
of a lonely pen
through the love of darkness.

THE ETERNAL TRUTH

As time ticks away
on another wasted day
the world's problems still stand fast
Win or lose? First or last?

And every time the wind blows
everything you did't know
turns into a revelation
and we stand in expectation.

The drop of gold
folds down your cheek
through you runs a shiver of cold
as life through you can leek

In the end it doesn't really matter
we are but a blink of the eye
and then our lives do shatter;
it makes me want to cry.

So as time ticks away
reminisce on your wasted day
and remember the eternal truth
that the first shall be last
but the last shall be lifted high
and exalted in the heavens above.

BROKEN CREED

At times when life is wicked
and I just can't see the light
a silver lining sometimes is not enough
to make wrong things seem right

Whatever life brings
I've been through everything
and now I am on my knees again.

But I know I must go on
although I hurt I must be strong.

The day reminds me of You
the night holds Your truth
the earth is a voice
speaking to You.

Take all this pride
and leave it behind
because one day this ends
one day we die.

Believe what you will
that is your right
but I chose to win -
so I chose to fight.

GOLDEN YEARS

From the coast of gold
I'm travelling far and wide
      But now it seems
I'm just a stranger to myself
and all the things I sometimes do
Isn't me but someone else.

So understand
Don't waste your time searching
For those wasted years
Face up… make your stand
and realise your're living your golden years.

HOLD HIGH

There was a man who had a face
that looked a lot like me
I saw him in the mirror
and I fought him in the street.
And when he turned away
I shot him in the head
then I came to realise
I had killed myself.

If your're free you'll never see the walls
If your head is clean you'll never free fall
If you're right you'll never fear wrong
If your head is high you'll never fear at all.

RESISTANCE

Roll me on your frozen fields
Break my bones and watch them heal
when I'll watch, I'll wait
and pray for the rain.

Seven moons and seven suns
heaven waits for those who run
down you-winter and underneath your waves
where you watch and wait
and pray for the day.

And if you don't believe
the sun will rise
stand alone and greet
the last remaining night.

RESTLESS

Even though its reached new heights
I quite like the restless nights
Makes me wonder, makes me think,
There's more to it - I'm on the brink.

IMAGES OF LIGHT

I close my eyes, I see a light,
a light almost tangible.
It stretches out like a road
I follow the road of light
to wherever it may lead.

The road is hard
the gradient steep.
I want to stop
I know I can't.
The end of the road draws nearer.

So tired
I need to stop.
Yet I cannot.
The sick equation of mankind
I can feel the wall to come.

The wall is transparent.
I can see through
the relaxation that lies beyond
But first I must break through
some doubts creep to mind.

Will I have enough to break the wall?
Seems so solid - so strong.
Did I spend too much on the journey?
I will need an untapped source of energy,
let this poem become a prayer.

OUR SICKNESS

The lie beckons
and we follow.
He opens the door
with a cusping hand.
We must believe to feel the high.
We've been fooled again.

Un - cross your arms now.
Take the offering and say
"I do believe".

We must believe
it is the only hope.
The only hope for redemption.
There must be a cure.

Betting on the cure,
it must be better than this.
Everyone has got to have the sickness
because everyone seems to need the cure.

People look for the cure
In everything they see
In sex, Son, or straying.
These cures leave the sickness.
I know the cure I will use.
The cure that leaves me secure
And so I'm betting on the cure.

ROLE

In my hour of need
On a sea of grey
On my knees I pray to you
Help me to find the dawn
of the dying day.

And in the afterbirth
On the quiet earth
Let the strains remind you
You defined me
You better think again
before my role defines you.

Nail in my hand
from my creator
You gave me life
now show me how to live.

And in your waiting hands
I will land
And roll out of my skin
And in your final hours I will stand
ready to begin.

ENDURANCE

A Wednesday morning writer
came wandering through the night.
We came face to face
(and she said)
"Bow to God's grace."

She made it very clear
that I must go on
though the end is near.

But it is a sad and lonely life
It's so hard to carry on
and I feel
that I'm the fool who lost it all.
I'm the fool, the joke of the age
I'm the fool who gave his life.
But this fool will carry on
this fool will eventually win
whoever shall be last shall be first
this is how I shall give my life
I shall take the place of the fool
the fool who lost it all.
The fool who carries on,
the fool who carries on,
carries on to victory.

THE PRAYER

When it comes to the time
are we partners in crime?
When it comes to the time
Hallowed be thy name.

God let us go and find what's to be done
Thy Kingdom come,
They will be done
on Earth.

Trying to justify ourselves, what we give
should we let and let live?
Forget or forgive?
As it is in Heaven.

But how can we let it go on this way?
when we know deep down
there is no other way.
The reign of the terror, corruption must end
No trust, no reason
No more to say.

Forgive me my sin.

ONE-WAY TRAFFIC

Sometimes I feel as though
I'm praying into a brick wall.
Your response is so slow
Are you ignoring my call?

I know You exist
I've seen your power.
Sometimes you watch me travel alone
As hour fades into hour.

As darkness continues to take
A firmer grip on me,
Please for Your sake
Talk, and set me free.

LIGHT MY WAY

A bullet is a man.
From time to time he strays.
I compare my life to this
to this I will relate
and I'm willing
to listen to your answers
and I'm not ashamed
to say I need you today.

So when I'm lost
or I'm tired or depraved
when my high bullet mind goes astray
won't you light my way?

ONE MORE TIME AROUND

It is all out of my hands
My future and Yours interwoven
Just let me go one more time around
One more time around that broken man

One more time around that shattered life
One more time around to give them hope
All I long to do is give hope to all
All I long to do is speak Your Word.

TO THE LEFT OF CENTRE
TO THE RIGHT OF THE WORLD

Bruised and beaten
cracks appearing
but still I'm not broken
little cracks
but I'm not broken.

Weakened but not destroyed
Wounded but not finished
Humiliated not fully diminished
so devoid of common sense
what it is to be enlightened.

Now you come to me
place your hand on me
no longer humiliated
no longer wounded
no longer weakened
no longer bruised
no longer beaten
but the cracks remain
as I am but human
they will always remain
help me to not let them widen.

YOU

The sun shines and I can't avoid the light
I think I'm holding onto life too tight
ashes to ashes, dust to dust
sometimes I feel like giving up.

But You....

You always reached out to me
and helped me believe
all those memories we share
I will cherish every one of them.

The truth is there's a right way to live
and You showed me how
so now You love in the words of a song
Your're a melody.

Just when fear binded me
You taught me to dream
I'll give you everything I am
falling still short of what You've done for me.

I've learnt that the world is bigger than me
Your're my daily dose of reality

You....

Your're God's gift to a broken world.

FREE

So much time I wasted
to be set free, it took so long.
Now hear my freedom song.
I've found freedom on your soothing arms
in all I saw before.

I saw, I said, but never believed
Now I see, I say, I believe.
I believe in you,
put my faith in you,
in all I have to say and I am free.

I plunge now into the super unknown
but not alone.
No longer alone in the super unknown.
I am bound to you
but I am free.

ALL FOR YOU

O Lord
could this be my fate?
Let it be
let me fight for you
let me take all that is mine
and make it yours.

My hands for shaking
          not for fighting.
I will not shirk the challenge
I don't mind the change
let me do all for you.

I am lost in the darkness
when I'm without you
I'm stranded in the mist
when I can't see you
let me see and follow.

I know I am heading for the top
and I'm riding you all the way
Your protective arms I leave for now
let me leave to do
all for you.

SURE

Time will take all of me
and throw me out of reality
but I know where I will land
calm and peaceful in your hand

I love the love I feel
when you hold me near
when I see you I can but kneel
and from me flows all my fear

But still, inside me, darkness holds fast:
the ranks of the evil one are vast.
It is (surely) not my fight to win.
He will take away all my sin

Passiontide,
Romanticide -
an angel on my side!
Christ is here to end this war
to deliver my soul from the sword.
Hope has shown me scenery
and I've found paradise in poetry.
Your death has saved me.

RELIGION

Oh people,
what have you done?
Locked him in his golden cage.
Made him bend to your religion,
Him resurrected from the grave.
If that is all you can see
Then he is the God of Nothing.

You are the God of Everything.
He's inside you and me
So lean upon Him gently.
Don't call on Him to save you
From your social graces
And the sins you waive.

So I asked Him a question
and he said to me:
" I'm not the kind you have to wind up on Sundays".
If you think
He is impressed by all your splendour
Then you'll be praying till next Thursday
To all the god's you can find.

I'M YOUR

I'm your truth
Telling lies
I'm your reason, alibis
Come inside, open your eyes

I'm your pain
While you repay
I'm your eyes
While your're away

I'm your dreams
As a stray
I'm your love
So keep away

I'm your hope
Just out of reach
I'm your hate
You cannot breach.

I'm your life.

I (do not) care!

THE FALSE FAITH

Your truth is hidden behind words
Your light dimmed through liturgy
Your flame extinguished
by those who would lead.

Can't we break away?
can't we start again?
Through the darkness
Your light still shines.

The rosary encircles the crown of thorns.
The Cross hidden by hate.
They've taken what You've done
and thrown it back at Your face.

You are the leader of all
how can I dispute You?
You are no frozen statue
I cannot walk around you.

WAR

Take a step back
Take a look
Death wears a blindfold
Carnage, undescribable.

(   )

Two armies so vast
Their ranks must stand fast
The bugle sounds, the charge begins
But on this battlefield, no one wins.

(   )

The battlefield is desolate.
The entrails of beaten enemy fill the plate
Surely will awake the beast
At the feast of the victor.

Reckless loss of life
Is always fun. Millions lay undone.
In the ant wars
For the barn.

REVEALING

I have hidden all my life
cacooned myself
Shrouded myself in silence.
But the weather has broken
and the rain will pour down
as the saturation commences
you will begin to understand me.

As the rain is freed
it bursts forth from the clouds
in torrents of truth
this is the freedom
that will soon fall on me
at last.

I'm standing in the rain
getting soaking wet
doing my best
but what do I get?
I try so hard to be set free
but once again
on the brink of freedom
the sun rears its ugly head
and just like that
the storm ends
and the rain once more
is trapped
held
hidden.

THE MIDNIGHT SUN

Father of my dreams,
shine a guiding light on me
for would I be here tonight?
If you had not forgiven me

You were bruised, beaten and rejected
all for us
who bruise, beat and reject you
you forgive us again

I can see you
the light in the dark
your noisy silence
faces the midnight sun.

My whispers in the night
reaches you in the heavens
and once again
You have forgiven me.

JUNE

Saturday afternoon,
the sunshine pours like wine,
know that golden June
can turn away empty grey
against your window,
and I feel like
I'm on the inside

If I walk by the trees
then I'll catch the falling leaves
and when the wind blows
you'll know all this means
because golden June told me
and when all else fades away
I'll be with June

Lying on the grass
on a warm summer's night
gazing up at the stars
blazing immorality
I see Jupiter
and turn my face away
He was just a figment.

But when I see the creations of June
I know it is all true
the shimmering streams
the peaceful lamb
the raging lion
the bread and the wine
all point to your truth.

Joy unsurpassable when I'm with June
ecstasy unparalleled
simply at one
unified under the sun
so here it all ends.

ARROWS

Bruised and beaten
Cracks appearing.
But I'm not broken
little cracks
but still I'm not broken.

Weakened not destroyed
wounded not finished
humiliated not fully diminished
so devoid of common sense
what it is to be enlightened.

So bring on your slings and arrows
I've taken them once
I'll take them again
so bring them on.
You'll wish you didn't
when I'm standing straight and tall
the slings lie by my feet
the arrows draw no blood
I'll tower above it all.

I'll tower tall
because I'm through it all
my enemies are defeated
as I stride away
I am finally free from it all.

But I know
Life still flickers
In my old foe.
It doesn't worry me now
I've beaten it once
I will beat it again.

HOMEWARD BOUND

Falling.
Spiralling.
Descending through time
as the clock goes round
seconds melt to seconds
and things will never be the same again.

I am not sure I understand time
so powerful it will witness the end of all things
there was time before me
and the time will continue after me.
How can anyone understand
a force so great?

All I am sure of is that
time will eventually gather me up,
keep me flying
and carry me safely home.

AUTHOR'S NOTE

Life is not about past or future, but a series of isolated moments like the frames in a film. Like the frames in a film, however, if one moment is taken out the overall structure does not make sense.

For example, in a film, a hand is going to pick up the ball. If the frame where the hand clasps the ball is missing then the entire section is ruined.

Does this mean that some moments are more important than others? Carpe Diem.

But who decides on importance?

Areas of importance can only be defined as important basis analytical study after the moment has passed.

So how can one seize the moment of importance if one cannot establish if a moment is important until after the moment has passed?